AF488408

CHIPPER

A Story from My Heart to Yours

Leanne Morris Gerrard

Illustrations: Elise Guidoux
Design: Karen Koshgarian

ISBN/SKU: 979-8-218-43131-0

First printing: 2024

Stellaleo Publishing
Camas, Washington

This special book is dedicated to my family:
In order to keep a beautiful memory alive
through the generations!

And a very loving acknowledgment to Laurel Airica who
is no longer with us physically, but alive and well in the
hearts of all of us she encouraged and inspired to write.

This is a tale that wants to be told;
Of a small baby bird left out in the cold.

A true story it is; about sixty years past;
So a book I have written, to ensure it will last!

Remembering Chipper with fondness and love,
Whenever I see a blue jay above.

I was just nine years old on that cold rainy day,
When I peeked out the window and wished I could play.

But when I looked closely, I saw a wee bird;
Alone and so helpless; in my heart something stirred.

I ran out to the yard and heard your sad cry;
I knew I must help you! I certainly would try!

Lifting you gently from the damp chilly ground;
I could see that your mother was nowhere around.

Holding you close, I brought you inside;
And found you a box, about twelve inches wide.

Mama brought some old towels to make a soft nest;
And you snuggled down in for a warm cozy rest.

You were so little, we could not even see
What kind of a bird you would turn out to be!

We fed you some bread mixed with lots of good stuff;
You fell fast asleep once you'd had quite enough.

We worried and wondered if you'd live through the night;
But had warm loving hopes that you'd soon be alright!

When morning arrived, you were so full of spunk;
You hopped out of your box, and landed ker-plunk!

You grew more each day, and became quite a bit stronger;
Your feathers turned blue and were very much longer!

Now that we knew, we finally could say;
The mystery was solved! We had a Blue Jay!

We thought and we thought to find just the right name,
And as we were thinking, my Daddy exclaimed:

"Chipper it is! It's just perfect enough
For this noisy and spry little ball of blue fluff!"

With my sister and brother, I ran through the fields
Catching crickets and grasshoppers for all of your meals.

We loved you so much, and kept you from harm;
But once you could fly, we had cause for alarm!

You flew through the house, chirping with glee;
You perched on the curtains and pooped in our tea!

The house was no place for a bird who could fly;
What a mess you did make, so we knew time was nigh;

You needed tall trees, and the sky to soar high;
So we freed you outside, and said our goodbyes.

You were happy out there, but you came every day
And squawked at the window for us to come play!

You took trinkets and toys way up in a tree
And hid them in places where no one could see!

From a gentleman's mouth, you snatched a cigar;
His startled surprise, we could see from afar!

You'd swoop from above, and land on a head,
Or sit on a shoulder and demand to be fed!

Among neighbors and friends you became like a pet,
With your lovable nature, you charmed all you met!

You gave so much love and brought joy to us all,
With your comical antics, I so fondly recall.

Then, one day you were gone, and we looked everywhere;
We searched and we called, and we hoped you'd be there.

But you didn't return, and our hearts felt so sad;
As a part of our family, you had made us so glad!

You stayed for as long as Nature allowed;
To have known you and loved you, I was *so* very proud!

Oh Chipper, my Chipper, you're still in my heart;
You'll live there forever, your home from the start!

All About Blue Jays

Did you know that blue jays are from the family of birds called Corvids?
Corvids include crows, ravens, magpies, nutcrackers, and all the other kinds of jays such as
Steller's jays and the many different scrub jays.

Birds who are from the Corvid family are very intelligent, playful, noisy and extremely curious.
They live together in close families, and take very good care of their young, until they're grown
enough to look after themselves. Sometimes the grown birds stay around to help the parents
with the next baby birds who hatch in the nest.

There are many different kinds of jays in all parts of the world, but only one type is actually
called a Blue Jay.

Blue jays have feathers of blue, white, gray and black. They have a perky
little crest that stands up on their head. They usually lay the crest down
when they're around their families, and are calm; but when they're
squawking or upset about something, the crest stands up.

You usually know when blue jays are around because of all the noises
they make. They have a great ability to make many different sounds from
little chirps and squeaks, to grinding toy noises, crackling sounds, or big
loud squawks. They can even imitate the sound of a hawk!

Blue jays make their nests with twigs, mud and small roots.
They build them high up in thick branches of trees. When the
mother blue jay lays her eggs, it takes 17 to 18 days for them to
hatch. Blue jay eggs are light blue or brown in color, with darker
brown spots. After they hatch, the mother bird continues to keep
the new babies warm with her body for another 8 to 12 days,
while the father bird brings food for all of them. The babies are
ready to leave the nest by the time they are about three weeks old,
but the parents continue to feed them for another month or two.

Blue jays love acorns and will stash many away in hidden
places to keep for later. They also eat seeds, nuts, fruits,
grains, insects, and will eat meat if they find it somewhere.

Blue jays live all up and down the eastern and midwestern parts of the United States
and Canada.

We lived in Florida when we found our little Chipper. He was so small that he didn't have
any blue feathers yet, so we couldn't tell what kind of a bird he was until he grew a little
more, and the blue began to appear.

My family and I fed him my mother's healthy, homemade, whole wheat bread, mixed with an
animal vitamin powder, and a little water. Then we began giving him tiny bits of raw ground
beef, with the vitamin powder. He did very well, and soon we were running around catching
grasshoppers and crickets for him to eat.

When he started to fly, we knew it was time to take him outside, and let him learn
to be a wild bird.

Since Chipper didn't have a blue jay mother and father to teach him, he was only used to
humans being his family, so he was very friendly with every person he met in our
neighborhood. It was such a surprise for some people when a blue jay suddenly landed on
their head or shoulder! But soon all our neighbors came to enjoy his frequent visits to their
yards. He was a gift of pure love to everyone who met him.

We all need to do our part to care for and protect the nature that is around us. The trees
and birds and wild animals are so important to our environment, and they help make our
earth such a beautiful place to live!

Here is a picture of my younger brother, in 1964, around age 5, playing outside, with
Chipper sitting on his knee.

Leanne lives in Camas, Washington with her husband Steve, and two cats, Stella and Leo. She is the mother of five, and grandmother of eight.

She and Steve spend most of their time caring for their beautiful land, which they call Sacred Path Sanctuary. They both love to travel, usually either visiting National Parks or their grandchildren.

Karen Koshgarian is a retired art teacher, and amazing photographer, living in Portland, Oregon.

Elise Guidoux, also retired, is a talented artist and jigsaw puzzle aficionado. She lives with Karen, and their two cats, Rickey and Willow.